Rental Property Investing

*Complete Real Estate Guide.
Everything Investor Needs to Know
About Cash Flow and Passive
Income*

Jeffrey Turpen

Summary

In the recent past, topics on investments in rental property have taken center stage in most discussions. The main reason is the belief by most people that investment in rental property is a business which is only reserved for the very rich. This myth further proceeds that without wealth it is almost impossible to own rental property.

The main purpose of this book is to try and demystify this myth by giving a step by step account of how one can go about the business of renting property. It delves deep into the major areas of the industry which most investors do not understand. It tries to help potential as well as existing investors on the best approach to operate and manage a rental property for a higher return on investment. Furthermore, it acts as a guide to investors on how best one can acquire financing to develop a rental property and how they can manage the property for maximum returns.

In view of the ever changing environment in the rental property industry, the book attempts to inform the reader on the various means available that can be utilized to update oneself with the right perspective of the industry. It touches on the importance of working with a team of professionals in the industry to make the right decisions regarding the management of rental property.

This book also lays emphasis on the importance of self-education as a rental property investor to be well conversant with the industry including how it operates and the best way of managing the property. It provides guidance to the investor on how he can be able to set the right prices or rent for his property and how he can improve his cash flow and passive income. It goes into details on the best approach to use when renting your property and how you can prepare legal documents for your own protection.

At the end of it all, the book attempts to educate the reader on the best way to invest in rental property and the best way to manage it. The primary objective is that anybody can invest in rental property and get maximum returns on investments.

Your Gift!

We want to show our appreciation that you support our work, so we have put together a gift for you.

Just visit the link on the last page of this book to download it now.

We know you will love this gift.

Thanks!

Table of Content

Introduction

In simple terms investment property is an investment that is primarily purchased to generate income. This type of property is one that is bought for the purposes of either renting it out or reselling it for a profit after undertaking some renovations. There are, however, some variations of this term. One such variation is an instance where a family decides to downsize or relocate to another residence. This property can become an investment property if the family decides not to sell it. Another example is where one purchases a house that hosts many families. The new owner might decide to live in one of the houses and rent the others. There is also another variation where he owners of the property might decide to be using the property once in a while or during certain seasons as vacation destinations. Certainly, having an investment property comes with several benefits. These benefits include:

Potential for double profits

An investment property has the ability to offer two possibilities for financial gain. These two possibilities include rent paid by the tenants to the owner of the property and the resultant appreciation in the value of the property when it is later resold. The rent can offer a good passive ongoing income to the property owner. There is also the possibility of benefitting from available tax advantages.

This makes investment properties to attract a large number of investors because they are known to have better returns on investments as opposed even to investments in the stock market. For instance, it is known that the stock market is very volatile and the risk of losing out on investments are very high. However, the rental property market is quite stable with high chances of rising prices.

Easy capitalization

It is possible to venture into the rental property market with little or no money for capitalization as opposed to trading on the stock market. One has various alternatives of financing which include loans that can be acquired without using so many financial resources. This, therefore, enables you to use your liquid cash assets for other investment opportunities.

FACTORS TO CONSIDER BEFORE INVESTING

There are several factors to consider before making a decision on investing in investment or rental property. Let us look at some of them.

Rental property versus budget

Investments in property are one of the most effective ways of creating wealth.It can also become a liability that can steal your precious time and drain away your hard-earned resources.

It is, therefore, prudent to have a solid financial plan which will reinforce your belief in your rental property business. It is advisable to engage professionals in the field by always consulting your accountants and real estate attorneys. These are people who will help your out to realize our goals. You should be able to know from them issues such as your liquidity, the status of your retirement savings, and if your investment property can afford you a decent passive income even if your cash flow becomes predictable. You should also be able to know if your rental property has the capacity of providing you with an immediate income or a long-term appreciation.

The landlord question

If your financial situation is sufficient to enable you to invest in rental property, it is important to consider whether you will be in a position of taking up the responsibilities of becoming a landlord. This is an extremely challenging position that needs dedication and commitment. The management of a rental property will demand a certain amount of time and effort. However, you also have the option of engaging professionals to manage your property. The decision to be a hands-on or hands-off landlord will be your prerogative. Nonetheless, whichever management style you choose to adopt you must always ensure that you are always well informed so as to perfectly understand how this business venture runs.

It is advisable to link up with local real estate and /or landlord groups that have regular meetings.

This will help you to gain insider information from professionals such as accountants, attorneys, repair specialists and many others.

You will be able to be up to date with matters related to landlords/tenants, rental/lease agreements, access to trade journals and magazines and many other matters that are related to the rental property industry.

The location factor

Investing in rental property will give you various options to pursue. You can acquire rental property almost anywhere. You can have a team of experts manage your property thousands of miles away as an absentee landlord.

However, a large number of landlords prefer having their rental property near them. This is because this option affords certain advantages. It is easier to make good investment decisions when one is familiar with his surroundings. It also enables one to have good purchasing opportunities and comparable values.

Typical rental property

Most people wonder whether there is a typical rental property that can offer an investor maximum returns on investment.

It should be noted that any kind of rental property has the potential of generating sufficient passive income to the landlord.

It does not matter if the rental property is a single-family house, a cottage, a high-rise building, apartment building or a condo, all these properties have the ability to sustain a handsome profit.

Rental property suitability

When investing in rental property it is important to consider what type of property you need to have.

Should you invest in a high-rise building or a small single family house?

The decision will depend on your budget and objectives. However, for first-time investors, it is advisable to invest in a small way. The reason is simply that it takes some time before one can get a stable income from his investment. During this period one is also obligated to do loan repayments which, in most cases, come from regular income. It is, therefore, good to invest in a small property which will translate into smaller repayment amount. The next thing to consider is where your rental property should be located. Should you locate your property in the city or the country side? Should it be a resort or a residential property? These are issues you have to consider to determine the suitability of your property.

SEARCHING FOR RENTAL PROPERTY

When shopping for a rental property it is always good to have a written pre-approval from a lender. This will act as a ticket to gain the attention of real estate sellers and agents. This is because the pre-approval acts as a guarantee or security that the financing will go through. It also has many other benefits which include:

- **Having the full knowledge of the amount of money that you can afford for the investment**
- **Having the advantage of getting the best bargain in the market**
- **Knowledge regarding the type of investment you are looking for**
- **Fast and simple loan processing after identifying your investment**

The main reason why you are buying the property to get a profit and generate ongoing income. This is something you should always consider so that you can seek for the best offer that will give you an added advantage. It is good to set your price range and target the most suitable areas for investing. You can do this by using Multiple Listing services by real estate agents or newspaper classified section.

It is good to choose active locations that have facilities for shopping, recreation, nightlife, culture and many others.

It is also good to consider about resale prospects and whether the property is in an area where it can attract tenants.

It is also good to focus on the purchase price and the rental income that it might generate. The property should also be in the proximity of schools and learning institutions. This is good for tenants with children and also raises the profile of your property.

It is recommended that you look for simple homes which is easy to maintain and which has appeal. In the case of renovations, it is good to do the work quickly and put it on the market as soon as possible. It is good to let experts do the marketing for you so that you can get a tenant as soon as possible. A good way to find a good property is searching for distressed properties which have been foreclosed and are in the hands of the lenders. You can find these in online foreclosure listings. You can also use the word of mouth in your search for a rental property by talking to potential property sellers and letting them know that you are in the market for the rental property. There is also a good possibility of getting a good bargain from out-of-state sellers by checking at the tax assessor's office. There are many other ways in which you can search for the right rental property.

Other methods include leaving pre-printed cards in people's mailboxes in a neighborhood that you are interested in. You can also do "wanted" ads on bulletin boards, local newspapers, groceries, stores and even community websites. With a well-developed plan, it won't take long before the search for your preferred rental property becomes a reality.

BUILD A TEAM OF EXPERTS

Acquiring rental property can be made easy if you work with a team of experts in your endeavors. The first experts to deal with include your attorney and tax advisor to advise you on the viability of making this purchase and also about the tax benefits that you may accrue.

Real estate agent

The other important expert you have to work with is the real estate agent. This agent is very useful especially if you have a rental property that is far off. Real estate agents will act as your representatives and keep you informed on the type of property you require. Here are some of the things that an estate agent can do for you.

- Will meet your property investment needs
- Provide important information on property related issues such as taxes, comparable values, building codes regulations, rental amounts etc.
- Help you to draft an offer on any property you wish to buy
- Acts as a go-between between you and the seller and helps in the negotiation process.

Appraiser

Another important expert you will deal with is an appraiser. This is a professional who is able to evaluate the value of your rental property and advise your investment is financially okay. Most lenders actually need properties to be appraised so that

they know if the property has the right value that can necessitate funding.

Although you can find out the prices of such property from newspapers by price comparisons, it is good to hire an appraiser. The appraiser can help you determine the current market value of the property you intend to purchase. He is able to do a review of recently sold properties in the area and do a comparative analysis of the same using his technical expertise.

Investment property financing expert

You also need an investment property financing expert who is able to offer you important financing information. They are also able to help you with issues related to mortgages and their customization to suit your specific needs.

SELF-EDUCATION

The ability to rent your investment property will greatly determine your success. It is, therefore, imperative to ascertain that your investment has the potential to generate sufficient profit to justify its viability. Take the initiative to know all about landlord and tenant laws by consulting with your legal representatives on laws and ordinances in your jurisdiction which are applicable to your rental property. A good example is the Federal Housing Act that prohibits discrimination in rental, finance, and sale of residential property based on color, race, sex, religion, nationality, familial status, or disability.

You can also use the internet to download forms an information online or visit your local office that deals with landlord/tenants affairs or the attorney general's office. You should also try and find out if your jurisdiction provides regulations limiting the amount of chargeable rent.

There are also instances where neighborhood associations, zoning restrictions, or condo associations make it illegal for landlords to rent their property or subdivide it into units. You should, therefore, ensure that you're your investment objectives are within the purview of the law. On the issue of appreciation, it is important to consult with your local chamber of commerce or your real estate agent to know the number of homes in your neighborhood whose value has appreciated in the recent past. If the answer is I the affirmative, you will know that your investment choice is viable in the long run even if it is still struggling to break even.

Projecting Your Rent

To reasonably project how much rent you can charge for your rental property, start by visiting the website of authorities that regulate the industry such as the US Department of Housing and Urban Development. This website can give you information that breaks down the average rentals in your respective jurisdiction.

The statistics are usually based on the number of bedrooms in a property and this will enable you to adjust your rent either upwards or downwards. You can also use the local newspapers by going through the rent section. You will then be able to track rents for properties that are similar to yours for a given period of time. This information can also be provided by your real estate agent.

CASH FLOW CALCULATIONS

To determine how much your potential rental property is worth and how much profits it can generate for you as rent, you need to calculate its cash flow. The calculations involved are simple. All you need to do is to add up our regular costs which include insurance, mortgage repayments, marketing or advertisement investments, property tax, utility costs that the tenant is not required to pay, and a 5% emergency or backup fund. All these expenses should be subtracted from the rent so as to determine your monthly cash flow.

If you intend to purchase a rental property that is used for the same purpose it is important to ask the seller for the Schedule E documentations which can show any loss of income on the property. You should then consult your accountant to find out if such losses can be claimed from your income tax.

An overview may show that one can claim rental losses if his annual earnings are less than $100,000.

You can be limited to the deductibility of your rental losses if your annual income is $100,000. On the other hand, if our annual income is over $150,000 you are not liable to claim for any loss in rental income.

Rent Your Property

It is important to find good renters because they not only safeguard your property but also protect and take care of your property. They are profitable because they stay for a long time and reduce vacancy time and eliminate unnecessary expenses. Studies show that it costs more looking for a new tenant that keeping an old one. It is important to motivate good tenants in many ways including a small rent reduction or offering some gifts. The question is where one can find a good tenant. One can use the expertise of a rental agent who is able to find good tenants for a small fee. You can also market your rental property through word of mouth or by using the classified ads. You should be clear and specific in your ad to save you from much trouble later. If you do not want smokers or pets in your house it is important to make the point clear. It is also important to consult your legal representative before doing the ads.

The best way to go is by setting your own standards and list all the requirements of the tenant and check them against the landlord-tenant laws. You should be able to deal with tenants with a good income and who have steady and stable jobs.

You should also be able to project the length of time such tenants have had in their last residence.

It is pertinent to avoid frequent turnover which has the capacity to affect your profits significantly.

Lease preparation

It is important to consult with your legal representative so as to get the lease prepared which covers both your concerns and also is applicable to given laws. States and jurisdictions have different restrictions regarding security deposits, rent amounts, and tenant rejections due to poor credit ratings. The lease is an important document which will act as your success blueprint.

Lease purchase option

It is also useful to know that there are other options which include the lease purchase option to your property. This type of option has the ability to attract a number of tenants who are able to handle monthly mortgage payments but not a down payment on the property.

The process involves leasing the house to a tenant who pays a specific monthly rent. This amount which is payable within a specific period of time is known as an option consideration and is divided into two. The first part of the payment is about 5% of the property's value and is non-refundable while the second part is the monthly payments that can go up to $300 that is paid together with the rent.

These payments are geared towards the purchase of the property at the end of the term.

However, if the renter makes a decision of not buying the property the landlord gets to keep the money. This is a very effective way of selling your property and ensures that you get your selling price no matter how the market looks like. This makes the tenants take good care of the property because they regard it as their own. However, many people think that it is not an effective method since some renters give up halfway their payments. To know if this method is effective it is good to consult your financial advisor or a local landlord association.

MAINTAIN YOUR RENTAL PROPERTY

The law requires you as the landlord to maintain your rental property to standards that are livable. Among the various requirements include having a property that has windows and doors with locks, a roof which is leak proof, a heating system that works. Different states have different requirements with respect to maintenance and repair responsibilities.

It is also your responsibility to keep your property in a good state to maintain its value.

You should, therefore, engage dependable repair people who will be able to prepare your property for your initial renters, meet tenant needs and also put the property in order for new tenants if your old tenants move out.

It is therefore important not to allow your property to stay vacant because you will be losing money in the process. In case you have purchased a co-op or condo, maintenance is usually paid for by your association fees.

In case your home is a bit far from your place of residence it will be hard for you to do some maintenance activities like repairing leaking faucets, snow removal or gutter cleaning. In this case, you need to make arrangements with a dependable handyman or engage the services of a maintenance company. Your real estate agent is able to recommend a good company for you. You can also use a home warranty service. This service charges an annual fee that covers the repair of all of your major appliances for a whole year.

If you are an absentee landlord, you can engage the services of a property manager. The manager will be charged with the responsibility of running your property, scouting for good repair people, does your book keeping and other important roles. He is also able to collect monthly rent on your behalf and can even organize for leases to your rental property. The property manager is able to relieve you of these duties but they have to be paid.

Most of them will usually go home with between 5%-10% of your gross income or more if additional services are provided. This is, however, a good bargain when you consider the amount of stress they would have relieved for you.

But you should always consider the costs involved, your tolerance level and work schedule before you make any decision.

If you engage the property manager it is important to break down all his duties and responsibilities in the contract.

LOAN APPLICATION

The rental property business is dependent on financing and it is important to include your lender as part of your team. Home mortgage consultants are specifically trained to interview finance seekers in a way that makes them understand his/her goals clearly. This helps them to make recommendations that help the finance seekers to develop their wealth potential in the business. These are professionals who can make you analyze your options and customize solutions to meet your particular needs.

There are a number of ways in which you can fund your investments and it is good to know your options depending on your budget, financial goals and needs. It is therefore advisable to go through these options with your lender so that you can be able to select the most suitable option at your disposal. There are a number of options that your lender can help you to ponder over.

Home equity financing

This type of financing takes advantage of the equity that you have for your primary residence to purchase a rental property. It is possible to borrow an amount that is equal to the value of your residence. However, this type of financing may be tax deductible.

Renovation financing

This type of financing is a one-time loan that equals the purchase price of a property that needs some renovation less the cost of renovating it. The amount is based on the higher value of the house after the said renovations have been done. This, therefore, gives you the privilege of enjoying the dividends of your rental property immediately.

Low down payment/ No down payment

These are options that make a home to become affordable right away. This type of financing allows one to pay for a property with out of pocket cash for you to be able to begin to profit from your investment right way.

No documentation/limited documentation option

This type of option is a smart choice for people who are self-employed whose incomes are not stable and keep on fluctuating from year to year. It is also suitable for people whose incomes are hard to document.

This flexibility excludes the finance seeker from the paper chase and makes his entry into property investment much easier.

Loan Closing Preparation

This is a four step loan closing procedure which will give you a general overview of what loan closing entails. The steps are as follows.

Appraisal

In this stage, your lender finds a professional appraiser whose duty is to determine the value of the rental property you want to purchase. The appraiser will give an estimate of the property by comparing it to others that have been recently sold in the locality. Lenders require the appraisal so as to ensure that the property that secures the loan will cover it in the case of any default.

Home inspection

It is advisable that any home buyer should be able to do a home inspection. In most cases, a home inspection is a requirement for in the home financing approval process. The inspection should cover all major areas of the home including electrical systems, foundation, heating and cooling systems, plumbing, roofing, and other exterior features.

Title insurance

Title insurance is of two types. One is for the protection of the lender and the other one protects the borrower from ownership claims on your property. These are claims which can be made by heirs of former owners, undisclosed spouses, creditors of former owners, or any other parties.

The lender will require you to buy the title property so that they can protect their interest in the transaction.

On the other hand, it is squarely your responsibility to buy the other title insurance to protect your interest in the property.

It is advisable to consult a mortgage advisor who will be able to recommend you to a title insurance company which will give you more information regarding this type of insurance.

Homeowners insurance

Home owner insurance is a necessary document that will be requested by the mortgage lender. This type of insurance covers losses such as fire. Burglary, tornadoes, and any other losses. It pays for damages that may happen as a result of these events. It also covers the costs of repair and replacement of lost contents. In case the property is damaged and becomes uninhabitable, the insurance is able to cover for additional living expenses for a certain period until the repair is fully undertaken. It also takes care of losses that result in injuries or their properties are damaged when they were on your property.

Closing

This is the stage that you go through all the final steps in getting the loan. It is important to note that all costs for closing should be fully paid. You will get to know how much you need to pay for closing from your mortgage consultant and attorney. This is important so as you can avoid unnecessary delays.

Conclusion

To sum it all, it is good for any new investor in rental property to get his/her facts right before venturing into the business that is hugely regarded as a business for the rich. Any investor - rich or not so rich, can invest in rental property by following the right procedure necessary to make it in the industry. Before engaging in the business, you need to inform yourself on what the rental business entails. You should seek information about the business by talking to professionals in the field such as real estate agents, landlord associations, attorneys, financial advisors and many other professionals. They are able to offer you expert advice on the intricacies of the investment. You can also do your own research by educating yourself through trade magazines, journals and other documents that cover different areas related to investing in rental property. More information can also be found on different websites dealing with the same subject matter.

After gathering sufficient knowledge on the business, it is advisable to consider several factors before you make a decision of investing in the business.

Among the various factors to consider should include the value of the rental property you intend to invest in and whether your budget is sufficient to afford such an investment.

Other things to consider include the location of the property, the type of property you should invest in, and whether you will be able to take the responsibilities of being a landlord.

You should then begin the process of searching for the right rental property.

You can do this through a number of ways including placement of ads in local newspapers, consulting with real estate agents, searching for distressed rental property that have defaulted, etc. You also need a team of experts who will offer you advice on different areas of the business. These experts include real estate agents, appraisers, legal representatives, and even financial consultants.

After acquiring the most suitable rental property, you should immediately find the right tenant for renting.

The tenant should be an individual who is financially stable and one who will not present problems in future. You should also set out your own rules and regulations which should be adhered to by the renter.

Maintenance of the property is also important. You should engage the services of handymen and repair people to maintain your house to the required standards.

You can also engage a property manager who can maintain the property on your behalf. By following this procedure you are sure of maintaining the value of your property and at the same time generate a reasonable income from it.

Your Gift!

We want to show our appreciation that you support our work, so we have put together a gift for you.

bit.ly/2u7pdNL

Just visit the link above to download it now.

We know you will love this gift.

Thanks!

www.ingramcontent.com/pod-product-compliance
Lightning Source LLC
Chambersburg PA
CBHW070935220526
45468CB00005B/1785